Rose Quartz Magick

Cast Simple Crystal Magic Spells

With Just One Stone

Cynthia Conway

This book is not a substitute for professional medical or psychological advice. These spells are designed to be used in addition to any necessary medical or psychological care.

ISBN: 1540513351

ISBN-13: 978-1540513359

Contents

An Introduction To Rose Quartz

In the realm of crystal magic, rose quartz is one of the most useful stones you can have. Rose Quartz resonates with the user's heart, allowing the stone to be used in spells that are tied to the heart, like love spells and emotional-based spells. Users can use this stone to overcome heartache, find new love, or bring romance and kindness into an existing relationship. It can also be used in non-romantic ventures, bringing more gentleness and kindness into familial relationships, as well as those with bosses, co-workers, or friends.

In addition, rose quartz is readily available and inexpensive. The stone can often be found at craft shops in a simple tumbled or unaltered variety - either of which will work well for spells. Many online retailers like Amazon offer the stone for a low price, and any piece of jewelry using a rose quartz stone can also be used.

Keep in mind that a single stone should be used for each spell you perform, at least until you receive the result you want. Using a single stone for more than one unrelated spell may mitigate the results you receive. For example, if you want to cast a love spell and use a rose quartz for the spell, and then try to use the same stone a week later to open your friendship emotionally, you may unintentionally find that the spells have become crossed, resulting in an unwanted romantic turn to a platonic friendship. Thankfully, since the stone is so inexpensive, you can easily pick up a handful of them and keep the intentions for your spells separated.

Introduction to Crystal Magic

Magick, in its purest essence, is taking a desire and turning it into reality. Spells use visualization, energy, and willpower to bring a spell to fruition. However, tools are also frequently used to empower, intensify, or hone spells to ensure success.

Crystals are one of the most popular tools to use because they both refine the intent of magic spells as well as providing energy to the spell. While you can use your own energy or the energy of the earth to cast your magic, relying on an external source for energy will mean that you won't be depleting your own energy stores and becoming exhausted in the process.

But why crystals? It's because crystals are ancient stones that in many cases, have been growing for thousands of years or even longer. They emit vibrational energy that can help to intensify the strength of a spell. Their vibrational energy isn't just limited to spell purposes, either: Reiki practitioners often use stones to refine their healing energy, while others use crystals and gems for the purposes of divination or scrying.

Adding tools to your spellcraft like candles, amulets, or crystals can greatly improve the outcome of your spell, and using rose quartz is a wonderful and affordable place to start.

Preparing Your Rose Quartz Stone

Before you begin using your crystal and cast a spell, you should take some time to cleanse it and get acquainted with it.

Cleaning your crystal is an extremely important step that helps to purify the stone and remove any negative energy that may have been absorbed by it. Cleansing a stone is a simple process, and can be achieved in a variety of ways. Choose whichever one of these feels right to you and know that your rose quartz stone has been cleared of any negativity.

The first method of cleansing is simply to wash your crystal. Under cool, flowing water, rinse and gently rub the surface of your crystal. Take care to not get cut if you're using a jagged stone. Visualize the water washing away any impurities, dirt, and negative energy. The longer you wash your stone, the more you should imagine it becoming bright and glowing with its own internal, positive energy.

The second method of cleansing requires sage. If you have dried sage that's intended to be used as incense, you can wave the smoke over and around your crystal to cleanse it. Similarly to the above method, imagine the smoke is lifting and carrying away any negativity that was present in the stone before you began to clean it. As always, be careful when working with flame or burning objects and practice fire safety techniques.

Once your stone is cleansed, take some time to become familiar with it before you cast your spell. Sit quietly with it in your hands and visually inspect it. Learn everything there is to know about it visually - its imperfections, how beautiful it is, and how the color shifts over the stone.

Then, run your hands over it. Study the texture. Where is your stone slick and smooth, and where is it rough and uneven? The goal here is to learn what your stone feels like as well as you know what your own hand feels like.

Lastly and most importantly, tune in to the energy of your stone. Rose quartz carries a gentle vibration that's attuned to the power of the heart. You can meditate or simply sit quietly with the stone in your hands, but carefully feel the stone's vibrations. You might feel the vibrations as a gentle warmth or tingling in your hands, or perhaps you'll actually feel the stone communicating with your heart. Emotions may come to the surface, especially if you intend to cast a spell that's tied to your own feelings. Don't be surprised if you experience warmth, happiness, or even sorrow and tears. Let these emotions flow and understand that the stone is resonating with you and this is a normal process that will help you to achieve the goal your spell is designed for.

One final - but optional - step you can perform to empower your spell is to charge your crystal before you cast the spell. Charging a crystal is a similar process to cleansing a crystal. While crystals naturally carry energy, you can use an external source to further intensify this energy, or to imbue the crystal with a certain element that you desire.

Thankfully, this process doesn't require any extra tools or money, and the charging methods that do use items are probably things you already have around the home.

The first method of charging is to use the sun's power. Using the sun's power is a good idea if you want to bring energy, vigor, strength, or growth into your magic. Simply take the stone outside at sunrise and leave it in a place where the stone can absorb sunlight. When the sun is about to set, go back out and collect your stone.

The second method of charging requires moonlight. Moonlight is a good choice for emotional spells, familial spells, to increase feminine power, or for spells that call for rest and recovery. Like the sunlight charging, all you have to do is take your crystal outside as the moon rises and allow it to soak up a puddle of moonlight. For increase potency, you can perform this task during every night of the moon's cycle, or choose a full moon to charge your stone for a single night for maximum power.

The third method for charging is to utilize heat. While rose quartz spells typically deal with the softer forms of love, like romantic love and emotional love, utilizing a flame can help to bring a little more of the elements of sex, lust, and physical attractiveness into your magic.

Flames can potentially tarnish the appearance of a rose quartz, so holding your stone in a flame isn't recommended. Instead, consider using hot water from the tap. Similarly to the cleansing method, you can rinse your stone in very hot water and visualize the heat being absorbed into the stone. Alternatively, you can allow the rose quartz to sit and soak in hot water until you're ready to cast your spell.

Now that your stone is cleansed, charged, and you've attuned yourself to it, you're ready to use it to cast some magic.

Rose Quartz Spells

Revive Romance Spell

If you're currently in a relationship that's grown cold or bitter, it might be a good time to cast this spell. The spell is designed to only work if you and your loved one both want to be together and your relationship is beneficial for you both, so there isn't any risk of unintentionally forcing a relationship to stay intact if the two of you are meant to grow apart.

Take your rose quartz and hold it in the palm of your hand while sensing its energies. Think about what your relationship is like now, and how it makes you sad, angry, or hurt. Allow the stone to accept that energy and understand that it will purify it and take away the discomfort.

When you feel ready to move on, think back to what your relationship used to be like. Remember the sensation of comfort, warmth, romance, and love. Then, speak this incantation.

Love is warm, love is sweet
Bring this relationship some new heat
Help us feel some spice tonight
If this match is truly right.
Remind us of what drew us here
And let that desire sound loud and clear.

Your spell may take effect immediately, or it may take some time. Feel free to repeat the incantation every night until you receive the desired effect. The stone may be carried with you, worn, or kept under your pillow to bring the warmth and zest you're looking for in your relationship back to the bedroom.

Beauty Boost Spell

This spell has two sides to it: one is to help others to notice your most appealing attributes, and the other is for you to be kinder and more appreciative of your own beauty.

Everyone has something about themselves that's unique, attractive, or lovely to look at, but it can be hard to focus on that instead of the negative sides you might find yourself getting hung up on. Try this spell to encourage others to view you more kindly and to see yourself that way, too.

With your rose quartz in hand, look at a photo or a reflection of yourself. Think about the attributes of your face or body that you don't like. Now, visualize those parts of your body blurring slightly out of focus, like light is bouncing off of them and making them harder to see. They're still there, but it's not the first thing you notice about yourself, nor is it the first thing others notice.

Then, focus on the attributes that you consider to be positive. Imagine these becoming brighter, sharper, and more vibrant. Imagine people meeting you and being drawn to your positive attributes without ever noticing any negative ones. Your positive attributes nearly glow with radiance that catches your attention and theirs.

With these two visualizations strong in your mind, speak the following incantation:

To everyone that I see,
I'll show the side that's best of me.
When I look upon this face,
My flaws are gone, replaced by grace.
Let my brilliance shine through,
My imperfections out of view.

This spell is particularly useful if you cast it with a piece of rose quartz jewelry that you can wear when you're struggling to acknowledge your beauty or you want others to see your best side.

Gentleness & Kindness Spell

Everyone has rough days now and then, but if you're finding that you can't control your temper, give this spell a try. It can also be modified to be cast on another person if you feel that they're losing their temper regularly for no reason.

With your rose quartz in hand, allow yourself to go back to what it feels like when you're getting angry and can't stop yourself. Think about how that feels physically and emotionally, as well as what effect it has on the people around you that you care about.

If you're casting the spell for someone else, think about how their temper affects you and others. Also, try to think about what may be truly triggering the anger, if you know the root cause behind it.

Now, visualize your rose quartz emitting soft, pink-colored waves of light that pass through the target of the spell. As each wave passes, it softens their emotions, easing their anger, rage, or upset. As a result, their mood lightens and they become kinder and warmer again.

Recite these words as you continue visualizing:

I/They can't control my/their rage,
But by this spell it shall be assuaged.
With the light of this rose quartz stone,
My/their normal temperament shall be shown.
Needless anger and rage is now let free,
By this spell so mote it be.

Carry your rose quartz with you for maximum efficacy. Once you or the spell's target's mood seems to have permanently softened, you can leave the stone at home on your altar or another safe place.

Forgiveness Spell

Letting go of anger and hurt in order to forgive someone can be hard, but it's also the first step to allowing yourself to heal and move forward. If you're having difficulty with this task, this spell can be useful. Rather than making you forget the pain and anger you're experiencing, it allows you to fully accept those emotions and let them dissipate, as they no longer serve you.

This spell can be performed simply with a rose quartz stone, but you can also take a couple of extra steps in advance to improve its potency. A good additional step is to take a shower or bath and visualizing the water washing away the negative energy you've picked up from the person who hurt you, as well as the negative energy you've created that's become stuck in your aura. To do this, simply take a shower or bath as you normally would, and focus on the feeling of the water on your skin. See it rinsing away the negative energy down the drain, and as you do so, your aura becomes stronger and brighter.

Now, with your rose quartz in hand, visualize the energetic field around you. If you sense any dark spots, smokiness, or impurities, imagine those being pushed out of your aura by the soft pink glow your stone is emitting. You should begin to feel a lightening of your emotions, as well. Once your aura feels cleansed, you're ready to begin your spell.

Hold your rose quartz and speak these words:

You damaged me and betrayed my trust,
Hurt my feelings and left me in distrust.
Now I must move on from this,
My feelings of anger I now dismiss.
It's time for me to heal and mend,
With forgiveness this pain shall end.
I hereby let your trespasses by,
This pain and anger is no longer mine.

Following the casting of this spell, you may experience some extreme emotions. Just let them come and go rather than trying to push them down. Once these emotions have been acknowledged, they begin to fade, and you'll be on your way to allowing yourself to forgive whomever hurt you.

Friendship Closeness and Trust Spell

If you already have a good relationship with a friend but want to strengthen it or become closer, this spell is a good choice.

This spell is particularly useful if you gift the rose quartz stone to your friend once the spell is complete. Think of it as a magickal friendship bracelet! The stone will remind your friend of your friendship, and the natural qualities of the rose quartz will help your friend to feel safe and soothed around you, encouraging more emotional openness and closeness in your relationship.

If you'd like, you can focus on an image of your friend to further hone this spell. If your mental image of your friend is very strong, however, it isn't

necessary to use a photo. With the stone or rose quartz jewelry in your hand, evoke the feelings you have for your friend and focus on how you want to grow closer to them. Then, speak this incantation.

Friend of mine, I'll not malign,
Allow yourself to unwind.
My care for you will never end,
Warmth and compassion I won't suspend.
Fill yourself with trust in me,
I'll always be there, so mote it be.

Harmonize Familial Relationship Spell

Even with the best intentions, sometimes family members just can't seem to get along. If you're having difficulty with familial fights, arguments, or you're worried about an upcoming gathering with family members who typically don't get along, this spell may be useful to you.

For this spell, you can use one rose quartz stone or multiples. The spell will help to harmonize your family's relationship and moods either way, but if you're experiencing particularly strong strife, try using one stone for every family member involved. If you're planning a particularly huge gathering, you can cast the spell once over a large group of rose quartz stones, or repeat the incantation for each one individually; it's your choice.

To begin the spell, sit quietly with your rose quartz stone or stones. Think about what's been causing problems in your family lately. Maybe you're having difficulty with family members who never get along, or maybe there's a conflict that keeps coming to the surface. Perhaps your family members have differing beliefs that are causing problems. Whatever it is, focus on the problem at hand, and the fights your family has experienced in the past.

With that in mind, hold your hand over your rose quartz stone(s) and visualize a pink wave of energy emerging from the stone. The energy can pulse out, or emerge in a steady stream. In either case, visualize the energy pushing the conflict away from the people it emerges from. The bad energy is pushed back, then purified by the stone's harmonizing energy and light. As the negativity leaves the people involved, imagine them smiling, laughing, and being happy and carefree.

With the visualization strong in your mind, recite:

Familial blood binds us,
But this rage has blinded us.
Harmony and calm is what I seek,
Bring my family gentility and peace.
Though our lives and choices range,
These differences shall not estrange.
Heal this family's frayed ties,
Bring my kin a fresh sunrise.

Weight Loss Spell

Getting to a healthy weight requires effort, focus, and a good combination of diet and exercise. Magick can't make you lose weight all on its own, but this spell can help you to stay dedicated to your goals.

Sit or stand quietly with a rose quartz stone and look at yourself in a mirror. If possible, choose one where you can see all of your body, or at least the problem areas you're most concerned about. If this isn't possible, a photo of yourself or a good visualization of what you look like will do.

Now, imagine yourself going through your day and committing to good habits. Maybe you turn down seconds, exercise more, or attend the gym daily. Just visualize yourself having total commitment to the steps necessary to achieve your goal, and as you do so, your body gradually gets closer and closer to your desired shape.

With these images strong in your mind, speak the following words:

This is not how I should be,
Healthy and fit is what I want for me.
Resolution and strength is what I need
To reach the goals that I seek.
This body shall change into the shape I desire,
With mighty dedication and strong willpower.
The energy of this stone will guide my way,
And with it I'll change how much I weigh.

Carry your rose quartz with you or keep it where you typically dine. If you feel like you're struggling to stay committed to your goals, hold your stone and tap into its vibrations and energy. It will help you to stay resolute and focused on your path.

Move On From a Breakup Spell

Getting over a relationship can be hard for both parties, whether you parted amicably or otherwise. If you're struggling to get past a breakup, this spell can ease your emotional burden.

This spell is best to cast during the full moon. You can cast it under the light of the moon, indoors or outdoors. If that isn't practical, prepare your spell indoors, and then go out and look at the full moon's light as you cast the incantation.

Hold your stone in your hands and feel its vibrations and energy. Then, tap into your own feelings and sense what you're going through. How do you feel, and where do you feel it? If the sense changes, either becoming more intense or weaker, allow this to happen. The rose quartz is already helping you, either by bringing emotion to the surface so that it can be released, or absorbing it so that you can move on.

After you've spent some time with the stone and have gone through the emotions that come to the surface, speak this incantation, preferably under the light of the full or mostly-full moon.

Love has come and love has gone
It's time for my heart to see a new dawn
Soften this pain and fear of closeness
Let me be free to seek wholeness.
Sadness and pain shall allay
As the moon's glimmer fades away.

Cast this spell every night as the moon wanes. Once the new moon arrives, your spell is complete, and your pain will fade just like the light of the moon.

Letting Go of Sorrow Spell

If you're struggling with sorrow due to loss, heartbreak, or trauma, this spell can provide comfort. Its magic will continue to work latently after you cast the spell, but you can also repeat the incantation whenever you need an emotional boost.

Sitting quietly with your rose quartz stone, sense the vibrations and energy of the stone as you did in the opening exercises. Then, allow yourself to experience your feelings without trying to block or ignore them. If you feel the need to cry, just let loose and allow the rose quartz to be in your presence while you really open up and let the sorrow out.

When no more new emotions are coming to the surface, speak this incantation:

The pain I feel is overwhelming,
My daily life it isn't helping.
The time has come to let it go,
In the here and now, I release my woe.
Now is not the time to grieve,
My emotions shall heed this spell I weave.

With the incantation complete, hold the stone to your heart and allow your painful emotions - especially any physical ache - to enter the rose quartz. Visualize the dark energy entering the stone and becoming a purified, radiant pink energy that's full of love. Your spell is now complete. You can carry the stone with you and repeat the visualization if you feel your bad emotions seeping back in.

Opening One's Self To Love Spell

If you're looking to begin a romantic relationship or want to get closer to a love one but you're struggling to, this spell can be useful. It will help you to open your heart to another, but also shields you from excess pain if the relationship doesn't work out.

Sit quietly with your rose quartz and physically feel what your fear of opening yourself to love is like. Why do you feel that way, and what do you think caused it? Go ahead and let yourself experience those feelings and the rose quartz will help to soothe and absorb the anxiety.

The most important part of this spell is to ask yourself if you genuinely want to open your heart to your intended. If this isn't your true intent, the spell won't work. Go ahead and ask yourself that now. If the answer is yes, go ahead and proceed.

Visualize walls surrounding your heart, protecting you from harm, but at the same time, preventing love, kindness, and closeness from coming in. Visualize warm, pink waves of light emitting from your rose quartz stone that touch those walls and begin to soften them. As they do so, the walls shrink or collapse, allowing everything you want to come through.

Now, visualize the pink light turning into a bubble surrounding your heart. Good things with positive intentions and energy pass effortlessly through the bubble, but negative, spiteful, or hurtful things bounce off the bubble and go back to where they came from.

With that visualization strong in mind, speak these words:

With this spell I unshackle my heart,
And give myself a fresh start.
Yesterday's sorrow is done and gone,
It's time for me to carry on.
With this spell my heart reopens,
I accept love from the one I've chosen.

Find Love Spell

Sit quietly with your rose quartz and focus on the vibrations and sensations you detect from it. As you sit with the stone, imagine the feeling of falling in love and the happiness you associate with it. Visualize the stone glowing with energy the stronger your feelings become. You may feel the vibrations from the stone intensify during this visualization.

Once your feelings are at their peak, say the following incantation:

Bring me love that's full of peace,
Make it so we surely meet
If our souls are to be bound,
Let it be that he/she/they are found.
Find the one that's perfect for me,
Bring him/her/them here, so mote it be.

Once your incantation is cast, the spell is complete. You may carry your stone with you, or leave it in a safe place in your home. In either case, the stone will purify your energy and release your intention into the world.

Ease The End of a Relationship Spell

If the time has come for you to end a relationship, this spell can ease the process. Whether you and your significant other are ready to break up or not, this spell can help to provide comfort, ease, and for each party to understand that this is for the best for both of you.

Keep in mind that this spell won't forcibly break up a relationship, as that would go against you and your significant other's individual will. Instead, if a relationship is meant to split, it will help the two of you to recognize your differences and distance and let the relationship go without pain and anger.

You can cast this spell solely with your rose quartz, or with the stone and an item signifying your relationship, like an engagement ring or a present you received from your significant other.

Visualize the two of you standing together, holding hands. Then, imagine that the two of you simultaneously let go of the other's hand, and go your own way. Your visualization might take a turn of its own - for example, you may notice that the two of you are smiling as you part, or that neither of you look back, but instead are looking on towards the future with excitement and joy.

Speak this incantation once your visualization is at its peak:

What we once had has gone away,
There is no reason now to stay.
Let us part without bitterness and pain,
Split here and now as the moonlight wanes.

Carry your rose quartz with you and prepare yourself to end the relationship. If the relationship is meant to end, you may find that your significant other broaches the subject themselves suddenly. However, even if they don't, go forward with confidence and tell them that it's time to move on. Your rose quartz will help to soften the blow.

What To Expect Once Your Spell Is Cast

Magick works in mysterious and fascinating ways. Once you cast a spell, it's best to let it go and allow it to do its work. Keep your eyes, ears, and mind open to new opportunities or strange circumstances that occur around you. If something seems like a strange and happy coincidence, it's most likely your spell at work. Go with the flow and let your spell do its magick.

If you feel that your spell needs strengthening, feel free to sit quietly with the crystal you originally used to cast your spell and re-cast it. Repeating the spell with your stone will intensify your intent and send out the message to the universe once again that you're seeking assistance. However, if you choose to do this, remember to stay focused on what it is you want, rather than concern or worry that it's not working. Focusing on anxiety, irritability, or disbelief may cause your spell to backfire and simply not work.

What you do with your stone once your spell is cast is up to you. You can leave it on your altar, or put it in a secret place, or even carry it with you to continue bringing you good energy and magick.

If for any reason you need to revoke or reverse your spell, gather the stone you cast the spell with and sit quietly with your stone. Visualize the same pink glow emitting from your stone that you saw when you cast your spell. Now, see that glow surrounding whatever the subject of your spell was; your lover, yourself, friend, etc. Focus on that glow, and gently pull it back from the target of your spell. Imagine you're reeling it in, and the glow and its effects are being drawn back into your rose quartz stone.

When the stone has fully absorbed the glow, say these words:

This spell's work is no longer needed,
What I say must be heeded.
My spell won't last one more day,
Its purpose will now go away.
The spell I once cast now is ended,
Its purpose hereby suspended.

Afterword

Thank you for reading! If you enjoyed this book or found the spells useful, please consider leaving a review for it on Amazon. As an Indie author, it will really help me out and will encourage others to pick up this book and improve their lives with magick.

If you'd like to learn more about magick, and want to be alerted to new book releases, visit my Facebook page at http://tinyurl.com/CynthiaConway

Facebook fans will be given an opportunity to be selected for free book giveaways and advance reviewer copies.

Blessed Be!

45552521R00026

Printed in Poland
by Amazon Fulfillment
Poland Sp. z o.o., Wrocław